H'm

H'm

POEMS BY R.S. THOMAS

MACMILLAN

© R.S. Thomas 1972

SBN boards: 333 13630 6
SBN paper: 333 13807 4

First published 1972 by
MACMILLAN LONDON LTD
London and Basingstoke
Associated companies in New York Toronto
Dublin Melbourne Johannesburg & Madras

Reprinted 1972

PRINTED IN GREAT BRITAIN BY
A. WHEATON & CO., EXETER

iv

CONTENTS

ONCE

God looked at space and I appeared,
Rubbing my eyes at what I saw.
The earth smoked, no birds sang;
There were no footprints on the beaches
Of the hot sea, no creatures in it.
God spoke. I hid myself in the side
of the mountain.
                    As though born again
I stepped out into the cool dew,
Trying to remember the fire sermon,
Astonished at the mingled chorus
Of weeds and flowers. In the brown bark
Of the trees I saw the many faces
Of life, forms hungry for birth,
Mouthing at me. I held my way
To the light, inspecting my shadow
Boldly; and in the late morning
You, rising towards me out of the depths
Of myself. I took your hand,
Remembering you, and together,
Confederates of the natural day,
We went forth to meet the Machine.

PETITION

And I standing in the shade
Have seen it a thousand times
Happen: first theft, then murder;
Rape; the rueful acts
Of the blind hand. I have said
New prayers, or said the old
In a new way. Seeking the poem
In the pain, I have learned
Silence is best, paying for it
With my conscience. I am eyes
Merely, witnessing virtue's
Defeat; seeing the young born
Fair, knowing the cancer
Awaits them. One thing I have asked
Of the disposer of the issues
Of life: that truth should defer
To beauty. It was not granted.

THIS ONE

Oh, I know it: the long story,
The ecstasies, the mutilations;
Crazed, pitiable creatures
Imagining themselves a Napoleon,
A Jesus; letting their hair grow,
Shaving it off; gorging themselves
On a dream; kindling
A new truth, withering by it.

While patiently this poor farmer
Purged himself in his strong sweat,
Ploughing under the tall boughs
Of the tree of the knowledge of
Good and evil, watching its fruit
Ripen, abstaining from it.

ECHOES

What is this? said God. The obstinacy
Of its refusal to answer
Enraged him. He struck it
Those great blows it resounds
With still. It glowered at
Him, but remained dumb,
Turning on its slow axis
Of pain, reflecting the year
In its seasons. Nature bandaged
Its wounds. Healing in
The smooth sun, it became
Fair. God looked at it
Again, reminded of
An intention. They shall answer
For you, he said. And at once
There were trees with birds
Singing, and through the trees
Animals wandered, drinking
Their own scent, conceding
An absence. Where are you?
He called, and riding the echo
The shapes came, slender
As trees, but with white hands,
Curious to build. On the altars
They made him the red blood
Told what he wished to hear.

INVITATION

And one voice says: Come
Back to the rain and manure
Of Siloh, to the small talk,
Of the wind, and the chapel's

Temptation; to the pale,
Sickly half-smile of
The daughter of the village
Grocer. The other says: Come

To the streets, where the pound
Sings and the doors open
To its music, with life
Like an express train running

To time. And I stay
Here, listening to them, blowing
On the small soul in my
Keeping with such breath as I have.

PERIOD

It was a time when wise men
Were not silent, but stifled
By vast noise. They took refuge
In books that were not read.

Two counsellors had the ear
Of the public. One cried 'Buy'
Day and night, and the other,
More plausibly, 'Sell your repose'.

NO ANSWER

But the chemicals in
My mind were not
Ready, so I let
Him go on, dissolving
The word on my
Tongue. Friend, I had said,
Life is too short for
Religion; it takes time
To prepare a sacrifice
For the God. Give yourself
To science that reveals
All, asking no pay
For it. Knowledge is power;
The old oracle
Has not changed. The nucleus
In the atom awaits
Our bidding. Come forth,
We cry, and the dust spreads
Its carpet. Over the creeds
And masterpieces our wheels go.

SONG

I choose white, but with
Red on it, like the snow
In winter with its few
Holly berries and the one

Robin, that is a fire
To warm by and like Christ
Comes to us in his weakness,
But with a sharp song.

THE EPITAPH

You ask me what it was like?
I lived, thought, felt the temptation
Of spirit to take matter
As my invention, but bruised my mind
On the facts: the old stubbornness
Of rock, the rough bark of a tree,
The body of her I would make my own
And could not.
               And yet they ceased;
With the closing of my eyes they became
As nothing. Each day I had to begin
Their assembly, as though it were I
Who contrived them. The air was contentment
Of spirit, a glass to renew
One's illusions. Christen me, christen me,
The stone cried. Instead I bequeathed
It these words, foreseeing the forming
Of the rainbow of your brushed eyes
After the storm in my flesh.

9

DIGEST

Mostly it was wars
With their justification
Of the surrender of values
For which they fought. Between
Them they laid their plans
For the next, exempted
From compact by the machine's
Exigencies. Silence
Was out of date; wisdom consisted
In a revision of the strict code
Of the spirit. To keep moving
Was best; to bring the arrival
Nearer departure; to synchronise
The applause, as the public images
Stepped on and off the stationary
Aircraft. The labour of the years
Was over; the children were heirs
To an instant existence. They fed the machine
Their questions, knowing the answers
Already, unable to apply them.

ACTING

Being unwise enough to have married her
I never knew when she was not acting.
'I love you' she would say; I heard the audiences
Sigh. 'I hate you'; I could never be sure
They were still there. She was lovely. I
Was only the looking-glass she made up in.
I husbanded the rippling meadow
Of her body. Their eyes grazed nightly upon it.

Alone now on the brittle platform
Of herself she is playing her last rôle.
It is perfect. Never in all her career
Was she so good. And yet the curtain
Has fallen. My charmer, come out from behind
It to take the applause. Look, I am clapping too.

11

PARRY

You say the word
'God'. I cancel
It with a smile.
You make the smile proof
That God is. I try
A new gambit. Look,
I say, the wide air —
Empty. You listen
To it as one hearing
The God breathe.
                    Shout, then,
I cry; waken
The unseen sleeper; let
Him come forth, history
Yearns for him.
                    You smile
Now in your turn,
Putting a finger
To my lips, not cancelling
My cry, pardoning it
Under the green tree
Where history nailed him.

POUF

It was March.
A wind
Blew. Sudden flowers
Opened in the sea's
Garden; a white bird
Stooped to them. From the town
At the sea's edge
Voices,
Frightening the bird,
Smirching the flowers.
The town
Was a thousand years old,
But the sea
Had refused to live with it.

PAVANE

Convergences
Of the spirit! What
Century, love? I,
Too; you remember —
Brescia? This sunlight reminds
Of the brocade. I dined
Long. And now the music
Of darkness in your eyes
Sounds. But Brescia,
And the spreading foliage
Of smoke! With Yeats' birds
Grown hoarse.
                    Artificer
Of the years, is this
Your answer? The long dream
Unwound; we followed
Through time to the tryst
With ourselves. But wheels roll
Between and the shadow
Of the plane falls. The
Victim remains
Nameless on the tall
Steps. Master, I
Do not wish, I do not wish
To continue.

CAIN

Abel looked at the wound
His brother had dealt him, and loved him
For it. Cain saw that look
And struck him again. The blood cried
On the ground; God listened to it.
He questioned Cain. But Cain answered:
Who made the blood? I offered you
Clean things: the blond hair
Of the corn; the knuckled vegetables; the
Flowers; things that did not publish
Their hurt, that bled
Silently. You would not accept them.

And God said: It was part of myself
He gave me. The lamb was torn
From my own side. The limp head,
The slow fall of red tears — they
Were like a mirror to me in which I beheld
My reflection. I anointed myself
In readiness for the journey
To the doomed tree you were at work upon.

VIA NEGATIVA

Why no! I never thought other than
That God is that great absence
In our lives, the empty silence
Within, the place where we go
Seeking, not in hope to
Arrive or find. He keeps the interstices
In our knowledge, the darkness
Between stars. His are the echoes
We follow, the footprints he has just
Left. We put our hands in
His side hoping to find
It warm. We look at people
And places as though he had looked
At them, too; but miss the reflection.

MAKING

And having built it
I set about furnishing it
To my taste: first moss, then grass
Annually renewed, and animals
To divert me: faces stared in
From the wild. I thought up the flowers
Then birds. I found the bacteria
Sheltering in primordial
Darkness and called them forth
To the light. Quickly the earth
Teemed. Yet still an absence
Disturbed me. I slept and dreamed
Of a likeness, fashioning it,
When I woke, to a slow
Music; in love with it
For itself, giving it freedom
To love me; risking the disappointment.

THE HEARTH

In front of the fire
With you, the folk song
Of the wind in the chimney and the sparks'
Embroidery of the soot — eternity
Is here in this small room,
In intervals that our love
Widens; and outside
Us is time and the victims
Of time, travellers
To a new Bethlehem, statesmen
And scientists with their hands full
Of the gifts that destroy.

RUINS

And this was a civilisation
That came to nothing — he spurned with his toe
The slave-coloured dust. We breathed it in
Thankfully, oxygen to our culture.

Somebody found a curved bone
In the ruins. A king's probably,
He said. Impertinent courtiers
We eyed it, the dropped kerchief of time.

THE ISLAND

And God said, I will build a church here
And cause this people to worship me,
And afflict them with poverty and sickness
In return for centuries of hard work
And patience. And its walls shall be hard as
Their hearts, and its windows let in the light
Grudgingly, as their minds do, and the priest's words be drowned
By the wind's caterwauling. All this I will do,

Said God, and watch the bitterness in their eyes
Grow, and their lips suppurate with
Their prayers. And their women shall bring forth
On my altars, and I will choose the best
Of them to be thrown back into the sea.

And that was only on one island.

HE

And the dogfish, spotted like God's face,
Looks at him, and the seal's eye-
Ball is cold. Autumn arrives
With birds rattling in brown showers
From hard skies. He holds out his two
Hands, calloused with the long failure
Of prayer: Take my life, he says
To the bleak sea, but the sea rejects him
Like wrack. He dungs the earth with
His children and the earth yields him
Its stone. Nothing he does, nothing he
Says is accepted, and the thin dribble
Of his poetry dries on the rocks
Of a harsh landscape under an ailing sun.

21

POSTSCRIPT

As life improved, their poems
Grew sadder and sadder. Was there oil
For the machine? It was
The vinegar in the poets' cup.

The tins marched to the music
Of the conveyor belt. A billion
Mouths opened. Production,
Production, the wheels

Whistled. Among the forests
Of metal the one human
Sound was the lament of
The poets for deciduous language.

THE RIVER

And the cobbled water
Of the stream with the trout's indelible
Shadows that winter
Has not erased — I walk it
Again under a clean
Sky with the fish, speckled like thrushes,
Silently singing among the weed's
Branches.
                I bring the heart
Not the mind to the interpretation
Of their music, letting the stream
Comb me, feeling it fresh
In my veins, revisiting the sources
That are as near now
As on the morning I set out from them.

REMEDIES

There were people around;
I would have spoken with them.
But the situation had got beyond
Language. Machines were invented
To cope, but they also were limited
By our expectations. Men stared
With a sort of growing resentment
At life that was ubiquitous and
Unseizable. A sense of betrayal
At finding themselves alive at all
Maddened the young; the older,
Following the narrowing perspectives
Of art, squinted at where a god died.
Between fierce alternatives
There was need as always of a third
Way. History was the proliferation
Of the offerers of such. Fortunes were made
On the ability to disappoint.

THE TIMES

There was a background of guns and bombs.
Bullies maintained their power
For a season. Cash had its say
Still in the disposal of seats, titles.

One voice, quieter than the rest,
Was heard, bemoaning the loss
Of beauty. Men put it on tape
For the future, a lesson in style.

REPEAT

He touched it. It exploded.
Man was inside with his many
Devices. He turned from him as from his own
Excrement. He could not stomach his grin.

I'll mark you, he thought. He put his finger
On him. The result was poetry:
The lament of Job, Aeschylus,
The grovelling of the theologians.
Man went limping through life, holding
His side.
       But who were these in the laboratories
Of the world? He followed the mazes
Of their calculations, and returned
To his centre to await their coming for him.

It was not his first time to be crucified.

FEMALE

It was the other way round:
God waved his slow wand
And the creature became a woman,
Imperceptibly, retaining its body,
Nose, brow, lips, eyes,
And the face that was like a flower
On the neck's stem. The man turned to her,
Crazy with the crushed smell
Of her hair; and her eyes warned him
To keep off. And she spoke to him with the voice
Of his own conscience, and rippled there
In the shade. So he put his hands
To his face, while her forked laughter
Played on him, and his leaves fell
Silently round him, and he hung there
On himself, waiting for the God to see.

EARTH

What made us think
It was yours? Because it was signed
With your blood, God of battles?
It is such a small thing,
Easily overlooked in the multitude
Of the worlds. We are misled
By perspective; the microscope
Is our sin, we tower enormous
Above it the stronger it
Grows. Where have your incarnations
Gone to? The flesh is too heavy
To wear you, God of light
And fire. The machine replaces
The hand that fastened you
To the cross, but cannot absolve us.

ALL RIGHT

I look. You look
Away. No colour,
No ruffling of the brow's
Surface betrays
Your feeling. As though I
Were not here; as
Though you were your own
Mirror, you arrange yourself
For the play. My eyes'
Adjectives; the way that
I scan you, the
Conjunction the flesh
Needs — all these
Are as nothing
To you. Serene, cool,
Motionless, no statue
Could show less
The impression of
My regard. Madam, I
Grant the artistry
Of your part. Let us
Consider it, then,
A finished performance.

SOLILOQUY

And God thought: Pray away,
Creatures; I'm going to destroy
It. The mistake's mine,
If you like. I have blundered
Before; the glaciers erased
My error.
       I saw them go
Further than you – palaces,
Missiles. My privacy
Was invaded; then the flaw
Took over; they allied themselves
With the dust. Winds blew away
Their pasture. Their bones signalled
From the desert to me
In vain.
       After the dust, fire;
The earth burned. I have forgotten
How long, but the fierce writing
Seduced me. I blew with my cool
Breath; the vapour condensed
In the hollows. The sun was torn
From my side. Out of the waters
You came, as subtle
As water, with your mineral
Poetry and promises
Of obedience. I listened to you
Too long. Within the churches
You built me you genuflected
To the machine. Where will it
Take you from the invisible
Viruses, the personnel
Of the darkness that do my will?

THAT DAY

Stopped the car, asked a man the way
To some place; he rested on it
Smiling, an impression of charm
As of ripe fields; talking to us
He held a reflection of the sky
In his brushed eyes. We lost interest
In the way, seeing him old
And content, feeling the sun's warmth
In his voice, watching the swallows
Above him — thirty years back
To this summer. Knowing him gone,
We wander the same flower-bordered road,
Seeing the harvest ripped from the land,
Deafened by the planes' orchestra;
Unable to direct the lost travellers
Or convince them this is a good place to be.

NOCTURNE BY BEN SHAHN

'Why look at me like that?'

'Well — it's your hand on the guitar.'

'Don't touch it; there is fire in it.'

'But why doesn't it burn you?'

'It does, it does; but inside me.'

'I see no smoke at your nostrils.'

'But I see green leaves at your lips.'

'They are the thoughts I would conceal.'

'You are the music that I compose.'

'Play me, then, back to myself.'

'It is too late; your face forbids it.'

'The arteries of the tall trees —'

'Are electric, charged with your blood.'

'But my hand now sleeps in my lap.'

'Let it remain so, clawed like my own.'

32

H'm

and one said
speak to us of love
and the preacher opened
his mouth and the word God
fell out so they tried
again speak to us
of God then but the preacher
was silent reaching
his arms out but the little
children the ones with
big bellies and bow
legs that were like
a razor shell
were too weak to come

THE KINGDOM

It's a long way off but inside it
There are quite different things going on:
Festivals at which the poor man
Is king and the consumptive is
Healed; mirrors in which the blind look
At themselves and love looks at them
Back; and industry is for mending
The bent bones and the minds fractured
By life. It's a long way off, but to get
There takes no time and admission
Is free, if you will purge yourself
Of desire, and present yourself with
Your need only and the simple offering
Of your faith, green as a leaf.

THE COMING

And God held in his hand
A small globe. Look, he said.
The son looked. Far off,
As through water, he saw
A scorched land of fierce
Colour. The light burned
There; crusted buildings
Cast their shadows; a bright
Serpent, a river
Uncoiled itself, radiant
With slime.
            On a bare
Hill a bare tree saddened
The sky. Many people
Held out their thin arms
To it, as though waiting
For a vanished April
To return to its crossed
Boughs. The son watched
Them. Let me go there, he said.

OTHER

It was perfect. He could do
Nothing about it. Its waters
Were as clear as his own eye. The grass
Was his breath. The mystery
Of the dark earth was what went on
In himself. He loved and
Hated it with a parent's
Conceit, admiring his own
Work, resenting its
Independence. There were trysts
In the greenwood at which
He was not welcome. Youths and girls,
Fondling the pages of
A strange book, awakened
His envy. The mind achieved
What the heart could not. He began planning
The destruction of the long peace
Of the place. The machine appeared
In the distance, singing to itself
Of money. Its song was the web
They were caught in, men and women
Together. The villages were as flies
To be sucked empty.
                          God secreted
A tear. Enough, enough,
He commanded, but the machine
Looked at him and went on singing.

THE FAIR

The idiot goes round and around
With his brother in a bumping-car
At the fair. The famous idiot
Smile hangs over the car's edge,
Illuminating nothing. This is mankind
Being taken for a ride by a rich
Relation. The responses are fixed:
Bump, smile; bump, smile. And the current

Is generated by the smooth flow
Of the shillings. This is an orchestra
Of steel with the constant percussion
Of laughter. But where he should be laughing
Too, his features are split open, and look!
Out of the cracks come warm, human tears.